This book belongs to:

_____

A

is for **Aretha Franklin.**
Betta R-E-S-P-E-C-T
this Queen of Soul.

B

is for **Bob Marley, Biz Markie,** and **Beyonce.**
One Love for beatboxing and all hail to the soultress Queen "B."

C is for Common and Chance the Rapper

Chicago's courageous South Side Champs!

D is for Diddy.

OR should we say Puff Daddy?
A dandy, dapper, and daring entrepreneur

E is for Earth, Wind & Fire.

Everyone, *Let's Groove* Tonight!

G is for **Gladys Knight** and **George Clinton.**

A funkadelic groove with a soul sensation.

H is for **Herbie Hancock.**

**A Hyde Park Alum,
best Jazz artist to have ever come!**

 is for **Ice Cube.**

J is for **Jay Z** aka **Jiggaman**, one of the best rappers turned businessman out of Brooklyn.

K is for Kanye West.

Chicago's best, a musical genius!

L is for Lauryn Hill.

Lovely lyrics that my sistas can feel!

M

is for **Miles Davis**, *My Kind of Blue*,
a jazz composer, that trumpet he blew!
Gotta add **Michael Jackson**
or Moonwalker Mike - The King of Pop
that everyone across the world liked!
Oh what the heck,
let's add **Mariah Carey**
and **Mary J. Blige**,
this would be a magnificent quartet!

N is for **New Edition.**

A R&B group we could never forget!
Let's give it up for
Mike, Ronnie, Johnny,
Ralph, Bobby, and Rick!

P is for Prince and Pattie LaBelle,
let's not forget to add a little production from Pharrell.

This supergroup would sound just swell.

Q

is for **Quincy Jones.**
80 Grammy nominations
and 27 Grammy awards.
Q is a musical legend,
salute to our Chicago bredrin.

R is for Ray Charles.

Unfortunately he couldn't see, but that never stopped him and because of that he never missed a key!

S is for **Stevie Wonder** and **Snoop Dogg.**

**Both savvy and smooth.
A Motown pioneer and West Coast King!**

T is for **The Temptations** or **TLC.**

One Male, One Female group. Both share a similar tune, titled *Ain't 2 Proud 2 Beg*.

U is for **Usher,**

who is super unique. At the young age of six he was singing and dancing to the beat!

V is for **Luther Vandross.**

**The only exception;
Because he's an outstanding vocalist,
a *Superstar* we will remember *Always and Forever.*

X is for XXXTentacion.

Our arms are around you.

Z is for Zapp.

The talkbox funk group that put Dayton, OH on the map!

So many African American Musicians
who have paved the way,
thankful for all even if we didn't say.
Please forgive me or should I say we.

Written by Lawson, Londyn, Dad, and Brittany.
This was African American Musicians ABC.
Peace out until next time!
Love, The Thomas Family.

www.ingramcontent.com/pod-product-compliance
Lightning Source LLC
Chambersburg PA
CBHW051150290426
44108CB00019B/2680